The Five W●rd Legacy

A book for living and giving

by

Noel Lockyer-Stevens

Green Magic

Green Magic
5 Stathe Cottages
Stathe
Somerset
TA7 0JL
England

www.greenmagicpublishing.com
info@greenmagicpublishing.com

Typeset by Green Man Books, Dorchester
www.greenmanbooks.co.uk

ISBN 978-0-9561886-8-7

GREEN MAGIC

CONTENTS

Introduction

How does anyone begin the impossible task of writing a book? Since I was a teenager I have wanted to write a book, but didn't know what to write about. Even if I did, would anyone read it?

So with such a mindset it never happened. There have been many things in life that I have never done, until I have. It even seemed that I would not be able to train to become an Interfaith Minister, yet in 2008 I started my training.

Perhaps the most valuable "lesson" I have received in life is that there are many things I cannot experience until I decide to experience them. Or at least become receptive to the possibility that I have a choice, no matter what stumbling blocks may appear in the way. Life seems to behave in that way; many things that would "never" happen in my life have happened (not all pleasurable) when I have dropped my inner "I can't" resistance and allowed the "I can" to flow.

Hopefully, as you read this book you will experience some similar thoughts and feelings. When you dispense with "I cannot do that" and affirm "I will try just this once", miraculous things may happen. That would be lovely.

Becoming an Interfaith Minister has had a life-changing effect on my life. It has been like a coming home and going out into the wilderness at the same time. Both places have relevance in our lives; both the familiar and the unknown can stretch our senses in all directions. The amount of stretching we undertake is based on our sense of adventure and being open to all eventualities, to live a life that challenges our emotions to the full.

Why develop The Five Word Legacy? As a Minister, I have the privilege of being a Chaplain at a hospice. Part of that role involves listening to people who are near the end of their lives. One person had an especially profound effect upon me. He had physical discomfort most of the time and knew that he was dying. His greatest sadness was that he would not see his daughter grow into adulthood. However, I had never met anyone who complained less about their life situation than this kind gentleman, who always had a good word to say about everyone.

While preparing to deliver a message at a Remembrance Service in late 2010, I went for a run to help me focus on what I would say. As the memory of this gentleman came into my mind, I wondered how he would be remembered when he left his body and went forward into the next adventure? The words that went round in my head as I ran are, I believe, so crucial in our human development:

Love – Joy – Happiness – Compassion – Kindness

What you are about to read is my endeavour to capture the essence of the above words and explain the reason why each word is meaningful in our everyday lives. What began as an "ah ha" moment for me personally, rapidly became a mission to share with others. Hence in December 2010, I was inspired to create The Five Word Legacy. It was watching someone near to death that gave me the inspiration to write this short manual about life and living.

Each word encompasses our being and is a legacy to live by. When truly felt and shared with others we are doing much more than "walking our talk". In becoming mindful of the effects of our every thought, word and action, we become conscious that what we leave behind, in every moment of every day, creates an imprint with far-reaching consequences. This legacy is not only connected with our own soul journey or about the legacy we leave behind when we no longer inhabit our bodies. It is a sequence of words that resonate within the hearts and minds of our fellow human beings and everything around us. Our greatest legacy of all is Love, put into action through acts of kindness.

My own intent and being open to experience acted as a catalyst in answering my own question. As a result, I have written my first book. Will you read it? That question only you can answer. I truly hope your awareness will grow, whether you only pick up and "dip in" to this offering or read it from cover to cover. My aim to contribute a small drop in the ocean of loving kindness and create a ripple effect will then be accomplished.

You will note at the end of each chapter there is an 'Affirmation', which you can absorb for yourself, it will help instil the message of that chapter a little bit deeper. I enjoyed writing each affirmation for each word of the legacy and life situation described within this book. I believe you too will enjoy the inner journey to be experienced on quiet reflection with each affirmation.

Thank You

With my sincere love, joy, happiness, compassion and kindness to all I have met and everyone I have known in my life. You have all been angels to me in some way, even if I did not know it at the time.

Those remarkable songwriters, John Lennon and Paul McCartney, are acknowledged for their wonderful inspiring words given at the beginning of each chapter, the tunes of each song are with me.

My thanks to Roma Harding who "edited" this text; actually she did far more, she allowed me to be articulate and convey with reasonable grammar the garbled messages I wanted to share with the world.

Appreciation also to Sarah Haywood who drew by hand the heart logo for the book cover. The logo was designed for a conference event we arranged and it seemed a perfect symbol for this book. Note that a single heart when it is open and alive touches the hearts of those around, who in turn touch the hearts of those around them, the blossoms of so many hearts are visible to the world. And so the cycle goes on, if we choose it. Sharing love is a choice we can all make, I hope on reading this book, that choice will become your highest priority to yourself and your world.

My greatest "thank you" goes to the undefined energy of the universe that some call God, Spirit, Divine Essence, or may acknowledge in many other forms. My name for this energy is "My Beloved", the big brain that gifted me The Five Word Legacy and allowed me, as the little brain, to bring this idea to you. I share here its profound consequences – the ability of five small words to change both our perceptions and how we choose to enrich our lives for the better.

With love and best wishes,

Noel

June 2011

"Lord, make me an instrument of your peace;
Where there is hatred, let me sow love;
Where there is injury, pardon;
Where there is doubt, faith;
Where there is despair, hope;
Where there is darkness, light;
And where there is sadness, joy."

Saint Francis of Assisi

1. What Is Our Legacy?

"But I just had to look having read the book."

from: *"A Day In The Life"*

We usually think of a legacy as something we leave behind for our family and loved ones when we die. Often this is in the form of possessions, the things we cannot take with us when we depart this earthly realm. This may be our house or our treasured possessions that had some meaning to us in life and then in preparation for death we choose to hand them on. Maybe a gold watch as an heirloom for a loved one or special friend, for example.

Does a legacy have to be something we only leave when we die? Another form of legacy is the essence of ourselves that remains in the memory of people after they have had an encounter with us. That encounter may have been brief or it may have lasted many years. The effect of our touching the lives of others may have been profound, or may have been the result of an ordinary event. For example, if I drive into a petrol station, fill up with petrol and then go into the garage kiosk to pay, I may have encountered three or four persons in that time. What legacy do I leave with those people?

For me, our legacy is the essence or feeling we leave behind for other people after some form of interaction, no matter how short or fleeting it may be, no matter how ordinary the encounter. Epiphany – the lights coming on and showing you all there is to see – can happen everywhere and anywhere, even in supermarket queues.

What are these emotional essences that we leave for others? There are many, ranging from negative emotions such as anger and hatred to indifference or disregard, through to positive warm feelings encompassing loving acceptance. We may experience all of these emotions in the course of an hour, perhaps from external sources such as being in a busy shopping centre or watching television, or from more personal interaction such as talking on the telephone or receiving an email.

How does it make us feel to be subjected to the emotions of others? Are we tossed around like a storm in a tea cup, reeling from place to place as a result of other people and their agendas or issues? Or are we centred, balanced and resting in a place of loving confidence; while all those around are losing their heads, we remain calm and at peace?

While the temptation in life may be to react to the influences of others and be caught up in this stressful drama, we may be better served by taking the centred and balanced approach to our lives. Where we blend both our essence of calm and our ego of action so that we positively influence and inspire the lives of those we come into contact with.

In her book *The Call*, Oriah Mountain Dreamer says, "Remember that there is one word you are here to say with your whole being. When it finds you give your life to it." Perhaps one word is all that we need as a legacy to the world. As you read this you may feel a meaningful word surging up inside of you; if you do, take that word and use it as your life's purpose right now.

However, I suggest that there are five words that, when linked together, can produce a legacy that brings healing to the world. Anyone at any time can adopt these words and thereby contribute to the well-being of ourselves and others. By "linked together" I mean there is a sequence of events that occurs when each of these five words combine to create a synergy stronger than any of the words individually.

This sequencing is about the feelings that these words generate within us – and in turn how we can reflect that greater depth of understanding through heartfelt intent back in our everyday lives. When the true meaning behind the words is absorbed into our being we are charged, ready and able to express ourselves in the world, bringing healing to all those we encounter. This is a bold statement, an expression that is likely to take the form of loving kindness; a new way of being that is so powerful that in working towards healing ourselves and those around us we can change the face of the planet we live upon.

This book endeavours to explain the five words, their sequence, and how they can benefit each of us as unique individuals. The life situations where they can be applied include work, families, relationships and other areas that may at times be considered to be difficult or conflicting.

Affirmation of my Legacy

As I read this text, I focus on my feelings within. I am not distracted by the outside world or allow it to tell me what to think and how to behave. I explore inside of me and I consider the possibility that I am able to leave a legacy to the world that I inhabit. That it may be possible for me to leave something of me behind when I interact with others. That my being can be loving and kind to my family, friends, people I know, strangers, animals and the world I live in.

I consider how I might feel about leaving a legacy that may bring pleasure to others and it makes me smile. I enter a world of possibility and sit quietly for a while.

2. Do Our Words Have Value?

*"Words are flowing out like endless rain
into a paper cup."*

from: *"All Across The Universe"*

All matter in the universe is energy. Some energy can visibly be seen to be moving, such as flames from burning material, but some energy is moving so slowly that we may not perceive its state of activity, like a house brick or a chair, for example.

We generally consider all living matter to be animal, vegetable or mineral. These animals, humans, plants, trees, rocks and crystals can absorb and feel an emotion as vibration. Subsequently, they will give out their own energetic vibration that can be felt by other forms of matter. Whether the response to this energy stimulus is positive or negative will depend on whether the vibration received is harmonious or discordant. An example would be playing classical music to house plants.

This allows them to grow into stronger and healthier plants than being exposed to acid house rock music (I think this is a form of music but I may have made it up). Plants respond to gentle energy in a way that encourages their growth but this is stunted in the presence of harsher sounds.

The effect of our essence or consciousness extends to animals, plants or even supposedly lifeless matter such as water. Dr Masaru Emoto in *The Hidden Messages in Water* has demonstrated with crystal photographs that water molecules are not lifeless at all and respond to conscious intent, words and music. He explains, "I have been witnessing that water can turn positive when it receives pure vibration of human prayer no matter how far away it is."

As plants and human beings are mainly composed of water, a similar effect takes place when we too are exposed to gentle or harsh sounds. As a being of energy, the essence of an individual person is likely to respond to extremes of energetic vibration in a "good" or "bad" way. In a physical sense this can be demonstrated, for example, by the pleasure of raw chocolate versus the sour taste of lemons. When we eat one or the other we may show the world what we feel inside by the expressions on our faces and our body language.

So as a being of energy, your aura or personality, or whatever you consider your essence to be, is also likely to respond to extremes of energetic vibration in a "good" or a "bad" way.

What do we mean by your "essence"? How does this differ from your personality or your aura, which responds to emotion and state of health, and can be seen and photographed as a coloured energy field surrounding our bodies? The message I wish to share is not however concerned with the complex subject of mind or psychology. There are many good books out there that examine this in depth. Similarly, the aura is a field (excuse the pun) of its own. What I would like you to focus on here is what you see as your essence – your own unique personal blueprint.

Some people call what I refer to as one's essence as their soul, their core, their centre, their inner being, or God particle. You can decide what your essence is called, how you perceive it and what it means to you. Is it related to your religion, faith, spiritual belief, or does your belief system give it another name? To benefit from this book it does not matter what your beliefs actually are. This is a not a manual about adhering to any specific beliefs or none at all, or what may be considered right or wrong. What is important is that you are true to your beliefs, own them and love and respect them as integral to who you are.

So your essence when you are alive and alert is open to receiving experiences, and through these experiences you are driven to react to the vibrational stimulus that you are exposed to. Let us return to the previous example. Visualise yourself sitting in a warm place in a comfortable chair with your eyes closed. You feel very relaxed and all is well in your world. Your breathing is calm, you have no worries or concerns as you just sit and be at ease with yourself.

While you sit in this relaxed state someone offers you two gifts, both of which you can place in your mouth. The first is a square of raw chocolate. Imagine it put into your mouth. As the chocolate melts consider how your essence responds to the delicious taste and how your face may look to other people. Will your face smile, be in raptures, display ecstasy?

The second gift, which you are not expecting, is a piece of sour lemon. Again, imagine what you will experience and what your face may show the outside world. You may consider one experience to be "good" or "bad". The look on our faces when we eat one or the other may show the world what we feel in response to the stimulus we have encountered.

Many of us may have witnessed parents or pet owners shouting at their children or animals to "get here now!" We may have felt the internal jarring of loud and harsh words spoken to a child or animal that has little ability to defend itself from such verbal aggression. We may have experienced someone in angry silence and felt the negative energy invade our personal space to such a degree that we cannot wait to get away from their presence. Some of us may have listened to someone describe a painful experience in such vivid detail that it felt as if we personally were experiencing their pain.

These are examples of how vibrations can affect us energetically in what could be termed a negative sense. This may "rock our boat" or move us away from our centre. Fortunately the opposite is also true. Equally, the vibrations of other people can affect us in a positive way. A state of being that is attractive and seemingly magnetic is because it is based in spiritual rather than personal energy. We sometimes refer to this as the other person's radiance or charisma and experience them as a powerful presence. It seems that they are more than just their body and mind; we gain a glimpse of their essence through being in their presence.

Taking this forward, words are much more than just the meaning they convey. We constantly experience their vibrations, which in turn create the emotion we perceive and provoke the feeling we experience. Some words can wound and sting, some can bring salvation and healing.

The Five Word Legacy takes five words: Love – Joy – Happiness – Compassion – Kindness. When used in sequence these words create a vibration that encourages matter to resonate in a positive way. They produce "good vibrations". Most of us would consider this to be beneficial and healing, and help lead us towards a happier way of living and a better world to live in.

The following chapters will describe each word in detail and explain how it can be used within our own lives. We may leave each word as a positive legacy for families and friends, colleagues, lovers, strangers, animals, plants and our environment. There is nowhere that you cannot use The Five Word Legacy in all ways and for always. Let us journey to the first word.

Affirmation of the Power of my Words

As I still myself, breathing softly and gently, I go within myself and find the being that is me. I feel the energy of the words I have read and feel how my own pulse vibrates to their rhythm. I do not use my mind to consider whether the words are right or wrong, good or bad. I feel what I have read as sensations and impressions and consider what the words mean to me as a possible legacy. Are they my truth? Do I, as a being of energy, within the shell of my body, vibrate to their frequency? Perhaps I am not sure yet, I may need more time to consider what I feel. That is fine. I prepare to read on, happy to embrace new ideas.

3. Word One - Love

"Love, Love, Love."

from: *"All You Need Is Love"*

Love is the first word of the legacy. It is no surprise to any reader that this would be chosen as one of the five words and most of you would have expected this to be the first. However, what love is considered to be will vary from person to person, so we may do well to develop some common ground about what we mean by love and its expression to help us understand why this is the first word and why the other words follow after love in this sequence.

What definition does a person give for knowing love? We know what emotions feel like, not from reading about them, hearing about them from another, or from watching films or television. We know what our emotions feel like from our experience of them (remember the sweetness of chocolate and the sour taste of lemon). But how do we know if two people have the same experience of the same emotion? In fact how likely is it that two or more people have the same feeling towards the same emotion? It may be that just as our fingerprints are a unique physical characteristic, how we identify with love (or any other emotion) uniquely defines our essence, describes the inner us – our inner being.

We may feel, think and act in a similar way to other people in relation to the same word, love, but in reality what we experience will be unique to who we perceive we are within our universe. If we take the view that each individual creates his or her own reality, which is influenced by conditioned patterns and issues that surround the nature/nurture debate, then our universe itself may be quite different to that of others, quite apart from how we see ourselves within it. The expression "it is all about you" may be truer that we realise.

When do we know if we are in place of love? Love is a bit like charity begins at home; it begins within each of us. Love is the essence of all that is good in our world. It is embodied in our unconditional loving care for ourselves and for others. This is not sentimental "Hollywood love". If I am loving towards myself and have healthy regard for myself as a living essence, I will want to take care of my inner self in order to achieve the loving and peaceful calm described earlier. For me personally, I am my essence first, my mind second, and my body third.

Why do I say this? Let's look at this in reverse order. My body does what my mind tells it, to stand up or sit down for example. But what tells my mind what to think? For me this is my essence. In Platonic philosophy this could be described as "the heart within the mind" or the other way around "the mind within the heart". But we don't need to worry about this here, just be comfortable with the concept of having an inner heart-centred place within you.

As an Interfaith Minister, I could say that what I consider to be my essence is driven by my belief in God, or higher power; it is what I consider myself to be, a soul being. You may have your own definition, for as I stated earlier, there is no right or wrong in this book. I would say however that my essence comprises of emotions and feelings that drive the mind, rather than the other way round.

How do I achieve a loving state of being for myself? I do it with a vertical (up and down) connection with my essence that I know as my belief. I remember my beliefs that I hold not only most dear to me, but also nearest to my heart. They are not shaken or tossed by the beliefs of others, but are integral within my life.

For many people that belief is known as God, Allah, Baba, Great Mystery or any other name that allows us to connect through our spiritual belief with the spirit within us. My personal word for my belief is "My Beloved". For others their belief may be represented by something else; perhaps a football team, an actor, musician, some other icon or idol.

What do I have to do to have this connection? Actually I do not have to "do" anything, but I need to remember to "be" me. By being me, I use what the book *A Course in Miracles* calls "The Holy Instant". This is using the instant "now", right now in the present moment without any delay. There is a sense of urgency about this need to act, not to allow a moment of procrastination to overtake us and consume us with doubt about why we cannot have this precious instant. Our minds may create many reasons as to why we do not "deserve" to be in this instant – to live in the moment. Perhaps we feel unworthy, or we are too angry, too sad, in too much pain, or just caught up in the drama of life that makes us feel too busy to be truly alive. Instead we live a lie that says we do not have time to live to our full potential.

Having decided to live in my truth, I create a connection that reminds me that I am powerful in my essence. I am then able to be sufficiently calm to feel the love I have for my belief and for myself. All else in that moment has no relevance because I am in the centre of my being. The drama and trauma of the day can wait.

For many of us, remembering to return to our centre does not come easily. To help us not to forget to do this, some kind of discipline or practice is required. How we do this is different for all of us. Remember that just because our practices may be different does not make them right or wrong; these differences can be celebrated. This celebration rather than criticism of our differences will be one of the most powerful forces that will bring change and healing to our world, because in order to celebrate we use loving kindness towards others.

We can start in the morning with a prayer to our beloved, a meditation to find inner stillness, an affirmation that inspires us, even listening to acid house rock music (again does this really exist?). If it works and is true for you, just do it! The important thing is to focus on your chosen activity and not to get distracted by the demands of the day ahead.

Throughout the day we can remind ourselves that we are still that centred being and just before bed we can give gratitude for having maintained our feelings of love for ourselves and for our source beliefs. How can we do this during our hectic days? Stop. Just stop for one minute every hour, consider it a quick shower to freshen up for the next hour, so that you remain focused and centred and able to love and respect yourself. When you concentrate on love in this way you will know that the quote from my youngest son when he was four years old is true. He said to his mum one day, "love is like space mummy, it never ends." Profound truth from one so young!

At this point you may be wondering why this is all about how "I" feel? Why is it not considering the feelings of others? Is that not selfish, aren't spiritual people meant to be selfless? Good question and there is a good answer.

Put simply, Jesus said, "love your neighbour as yourself." In order to give genuine love to another I need to have received genuine love from my source. To give loving kindness to others, I must know how to give love to myself, otherwise I am going to deplete myself very soon and people around me will be affected by my lack of self-love. Everyone notices how we feel; we cannot fake it for long. To give is to receive and vice versa.

The following words from the Sufi poet Rumi help explain this connection:

> *O Love, O pure deep Love, be here, be now*
> *Be all; worlds dissolve in your endless stainless radiance*
> *Frail living leaves burn with you brighter than cold stars*
> *Make me your servant, your breath, your core.*

Rumi asks for Love to make him his servant, to serve the call of love brought to him by his beloved. There is no selfishness in that request, he is asking for love to be present within him so that he can serve the world. Such service is performed in a state of bliss not servitude. In bliss you are ready to be truly remarkable in your life and live to your magnificent full potential.

So you consider yourself to be an important person in your life and have achieved inner love, connected with your source, and realised what you believe and hold dear and true. You have given yourself permission to receive love from yourself – and the truth within you – for yourself. The first word of the legacy has been achieved.

What happens next? The second word of The Five Word Legacy.

Affirmation of Love

I am a being of energy. I am aware that the way I respond to the love I feel for myself, working on the inside of me, acts as a vibration that makes me feel lighter. I am no longer burdened by my usual worries of the world.

I know that I can love myself without arrogance or guilt, that with self-love I can prepare myself to give a loving legacy to my world and those within it. I feel a tingle of a new experience starting to fill me, a glow and an awakening to the possibility that I can bring healing to myself and all things and beings that I connect with in my world.

4. Word Two - Joy

"One, two, three, four, can I have a little more?"

from: *"All Together Now"*

What does joy feel like? Like love it can be subjective and open to our individual interpretation. Try to remember experiences that made you joyful. Were they childhood events, a wedding to your sweetheart, the birth of a child, gaining a qualification, buying a house, being in love with someone?

If you have chosen one of the above events, then you are looking at love on the outside of you, believing what you feel is joy. For the purpose of the legacy it could be that what you experienced as a feeling was happiness, not joy; you received it because of someone or something external to you. As we know, when we are centred beings we receive love from within. So where does joy come from?

I believe that joy is an internal sensation and that it is received in the vertical plane (again, up and down) of the joy of knowing that I am love and have the ability to be loving. Joy then is an inner radiance that I have because I am aware of a love of love and a love of life that prepares me to give and receive without measure.

This joy is within me as a gift given to me by the universe, a state of being that glows within. I say that this gift is given to me by the universe, because no person can give me this joy, it is mine to be discovered because I have discovered love from within me. This joy is the reassurance that all is well and that all will be well.

Psalm 46 from The Old Testament says, "Be still and know that I am God." If this means that I know I have the experience of joy because of the love of my belief within me, then how blessed am I within my daily life?

What is there to be joyful about? Our world shows us many aspects of life that we may neither like nor agree with. When we watch television we may see many scenes that distress us. We may like football and dislike rugby, and be upset if our favourite team does not win, but neither should bring us sadness unless we choose to allow sadness to enter. Yet for many there are external influences that allow events and other people to take our joy and replace it with sorrow. The car would not start, a news item upsets us, in a relationship harsh words can wound, a comment made at work or at school may unsettle us.

Sometimes the most powerful feelings of sadness are caused by memories of the past or our fears of the future. Joy is the knowledge that even in sadness we can access a feeling in every cell of our bodies that is able to bring us hope. This is the joy of the love of being alive.

So joy is on the inside of us. It is the fire of the soul fuelled by love and nestles in the fireplace of courage – the courage to be joy despite the external influences and injustices of the world. This courage to be joyful no matter what we may witness, the knowing

18

that everything external in life changes, is shown in the Buddhist proverb that "this too will pass."

That means two things. First, that everything changes; life is not static. Our acceptance of that fact helps us to reduce the level of attachment that we may have to possessions and situations, knowing that these will change at some time in the future. We may gain more possessions and we may lose some. Our jobs, our homes, our relationships may change from where they are now. Our belief system may say that change is either good or bad for us. Our acceptance of the journey that we are on is as important as any destination we may reach in our life's travels; acceptance allows us to remain in our loving and joyful centre of being. We observe what goes on around us, but with a sense of loving non-attachment to the fear of losing what we have accumulated for ourselves, so that we can live without fear of loss.

The second thing is this. Even if we have a million pounds in the bank, one day we may not have that money, because "this too will pass." If we attach ourselves to the fear of loss, we are haunted on a daily basis, we may even attract the loss as a self-fulfilling prophecy, ensuring the million pounds is lost. Then we suffer not only the process of the loss, but also the consequent outcome of the loss. Pain and suffering are likely to be the emotions we feel, our joy of life given away to the fear of loss.

Now we have two of the five words to our legacy. It is important to recognise that both are internal or, to use the phrase, they are "all about us". They are about making sure that we have taken care of ourselves, lovingly and joyfully, so that we can prepare for the next three words of The Five Word Legacy. These are all about how we share our love and joy with the world.

Affirmation for Joy

It becomes easier for me to go within myself. The words I read are special and act as an awakening of old feelings, some I have not felt since I was very, very young. As I concentrate on the inner me, I am rewarded with the joy of knowing that I am a being of love. I know that having experienced such deep inner love for myself, the feeling that follows is one of joy and that I can have it whenever I want. It is like a refreshing shower of wonderful feelings that I can have whenever I choose.

I consider what I need to do to choose to experience joy. I take the time to stop and let go of my usual preoccupations. I breathe slowly and deeply, close my eyes and look for the truth within me. The truth of my self-love fills me with joy for myself and for my place in the world. As I move away from negativity and doubt, feelings of guilt or fear can be brushed away. I am just able to "be still and know" .... that the truth of love is my choice to own. Why would I give up the joy of that feeling, when I can feel this good?

5. Word Three - Happiness

"I need to laugh and when the sun is out, I've got something to laugh about."

from: *"Good Day Sunshine"*

How does our love and joy make its way in the world? It does so by our becoming an external expression of happiness. We behave on the horizontal (side to side) plane of our being, through our interaction with other worldly matter. This is often most apparent in our relationships with other people.

We do not need to know we are happy, we already know that we have inner love and joy. For others who encounter us, what do they know about us? We may be smiling, our voice may be uplifted, our words kind and cheerful. The way in which we carry ourselves may appear lighter than air and we have a "Ready Brek" glow for all to see.

As like attracts like, happiness will attract happiness. Similarly happy people will want to seek us out and spend time with us,

21

just for the knowing of us and the mutual exchange of happy energy fed by the love and joy within both parties. We provide the external happiness for people, not love and joy, but now something quite remarkable happens. Our happiness acts as the spark to allow others to find their own love and joy. When this happens that which we felt may have been all about serving us, actually becomes all about serving others.

We go through a process of identifying our self as a loving being and in our state of joy, share happiness with people and exchange this happy energy between ourselves. This sounds quite easy, fun even – to leave a legacy of love and joy with happy people.

However, this too shall pass. The reality may be that we lose our spiritual centre and do not always project this love and joy via our external happiness. Or that the person we share happiness with becomes unhappy. Remember the storm in the tea cup that bobs us up and down, side to side, so that we do not know which way is up? In that state of being we are far removed from our centre and unable to serve ourselves or others. What do we do then? We can refocus on undertaking spiritual practice to return to our centre. Easily said in a book and may feel harder to do on the day you are made redundant, a loved one dies, someone leaves you or you hear terrible news.

The resource we can draw on is courage, the courage to remain happy with who you are and your place in the world even when the world and its events bring sadness and pain. Pain and suffering are "out there" to be witnessed all the time, but remember that responding with more pain and suffering is not a solution. The solution is to remain happy despite the sadness we may even feel ourselves. Keep the sadness and pain "out there" and allow the love and joy to remain "in here" – within you.

This is why courage is so important in relation to being happy; love and joy enables you to be happy and being happy allows you to be loving and joyful. To be happy requires courage and practice.

That is the truth of remembering who we are and the legacy we leave behind. From our centre we leave a legacy of happiness for others. However, to do this we need to "be" love and joy. Any road that cannot take us to this destination is of little use on our life's journey. Mohandas Gandhi reminds us, "Happiness is when what you think, what you say, and what you do are in harmony."

What is our purpose through our legacy? To leave an impression of who we are with others we do not have time to waste in not being our true selves, we have a service to perform in the time we have in the world. Like the White Rabbit from *Alice in Wonderland*, we do not want to be late for our entrance onto the stage of other people's drama. When we are called to play our healing role, we want to be in the right place at the right time. That is to be with the person or attend to the activity that needs our support or attention the most.

The third word of our legacy is an external state of being, spreading our love and joy to others via our happiness so that they too can tune in to their higher plane of being and join "The Five Word Legacy Club". The more we care for the happiness of others, the more our own sense of well-being is enhanced and the more laughter we can share.

To be happy when we do not feel we are, or want to be, may sound hard enough, but I know you are up for the challenge of showing your happiness to the world. To be happy when all around is in despair takes courage, but you can be a saviour of the world. So please get ready to be happy, because the fourth legacy word will require both courage and happiness, and for many a new way of looking at the world.

Affirmation for Happiness

I am quick to recognise my inner feelings of love and joy. They are easy to find within me. My resistance to being worthy enough to feel such uplifting emotions has diminished; situations with others that make me feel unworthy or unhappy now brush off me easily and readily.

I now know that my place in the world is to demonstrate happiness to others and present myself in a positive way, even in the face of adversity. I know that there are events in the world of which I do not approve, but I know that the love and joy within my being will help bring positive healing to the world around me. I become the change that I want to see in the world.

6. Word Four - Compassion

*"And when the broken hearted people
living in the world agree...."*

from: *"Let It Be"*

As we view the world through the eyes of happy people, we can accept that the world may not be perfect, or as we would wish to see it. Happy and unhappy people can see a world that is unjust. Both can see injustice through abuse of others, animals and the environment. The media churns out via our radios, televisions, computers and newspapers things that are happening that cause harm or fear to others. Sometimes all we can do is watch and know that such events exist, sometimes we can take positive action to reduce fear and harm in the lives of others, sometimes we can make small gestures that protect our environment and the beautiful planet gifted to us all.

How can happy people project themselves towards others

in a way that is of spiritual service? In the same way as we show happiness to others, compassion is directed on the horizontal plane (side to side). It means viewing the world without judgement about what is right or wrong, good or bad. Compassion is the ability to be non-judgemental in all situations. Not to give in to criticism or allocate fault and blame, but to show mercy. As the Buddha put it, "to live with sympathy for all living beings without exception."

This is not easy because we are taught from a very young age to make some form of judgement about things on a regular basis. Whether it is a vote for a contestant on a reality show like X Factor or a judgement to stone a person to death for adultery, judgements both personal and collective are constantly being made. I may say that stoning to death for an act of adultery is severe, ungodly and wrong. Another person may hold the opposite view, feeling that a contestant on X Factor should be stoned for poor singing. Who is right and who is wrong? Both? Neither? Only one of us? If so, which one? This kind of issue is a minefield based on subjective viewpoint. Murder is considered wrong in the world we live in, but in some countries the death penalty is given to those who commit murder. Is this the best way to demonstrate compassion?

Please ask yourself who chooses in your life what is "good" or "bad", "right" or "wrong"? These are choices and in many parts of the world we are permitted to make choices through freedom of speech and freedom of expression. Others may not agree with such a choice and that is their choice also. Sometimes however we may feel that we should conform to what is deemed acceptable in our own society. Spend a moment to consider those people in the world who are not able to freely express

26

themselves because of some form of oppression or restriction that may prevent them living their beliefs.

Do we walk past a homeless person and pass judgement that they are only living rough and begging on the streets because of something they did wrong, or decided not to have a job and a home? Someone addicted to heroin, or alcohol or is obese through addiction to food; again did some weakness in that person (that we of course do not have) lead them to become an addict? It must be their fault so they are not worthy of compassion, but sufficiently unworthy to receive our judgement.

If you were to see a picture of a large man with a stick beating a small woman, where would your compassion lie? Certainly the woman would deserve compassion as she is being harmed and is the apparent victim in this situation. Feeling compassion towards the woman does however involve judgement of the man who is the perpetrator of violence towards someone who cannot defend herself.

Think of your legacy as a loving being, full of joy and happy to be in the world, no matter how cruel or harsh it may appear. The woman is our soul sister, the man our soul brother. Souls do not judge one another – there is nothing (no thing) to judge. Our role through our legacy is to offer compassion to both in equal measure, not to consider just one as worthy of more compassion than another. If we do not offer equal compassion, we are judging members of our own soul family.

Why should we change judgement for compassion? As we view the current state of our world, can we say that our judgements have made the world a better place to live, that it is filled with happiness, that everywhere we look we see expressions of love and joy?

People with compassion, while not condoning violence, will not judge, nor will they be complacent about the need to make changes that reduce abuse and cruelty. Compassion is a gentle view, a way of looking at all situations, not wanting to be harsh but to find a way to bring healing.

If we are not prepared to take responsibility for our words and actions we will ultimately blame others, whether it is something we don't like in society or when something goes wrong in our personal lives. This can happen when fear takes hold of us. Can we go within and recognise, "the reason that just happened is because I allowed inner fear to find another to take the blame for how I feel?" While others may influence us, the reality is that if I do not like what I feel, I need to find a way to bring about my change.

By changing our view of the world we will bring about the change we want to see. Mohandas Gandhi said this long before he died. He may have been right, but it takes a critical mass of people to start this off, to get others to follow us towards a loving legacy that displays compassion and mercy towards even the most brutal of acts. Brutal retaliation towards brutality breeds more brutality. If we want a compassionate world to live in, we cannot judge how it works as right or wrong. The choice we can make is one of discernment rather than judgement.

Apply a simple test and ask, "does this choice serve the world I live in without harming it?" If the answer is yes you are using compassion to make the best decision you are able. If the answer is no then choose again. We will do well to also remember to show compassion for ourselves, not just extend it towards others or elsewhere. If we can only ask ourselves, from our place of love and joy, if our choice in any given moment serves the "highest good", the world would be a happier place.

So as a challenge for you, the reader, do you find yourself judging people and situations, and can you accept the judgement of others? Or can you give and receive compassion in equal amounts always and in all ways?

If you can do this, then four words of the legacy are understood. We can only attempt to bring about the change we want to see in the world through our own thoughts, feelings and actions. The words of the legacy are a tool to help us do this by encouraging us to change our view of the world. These words encourage us to be inspired and have the confidence to love ourselves, love others, encompass joy and be happy. Thus we create good vibrations around us, have more fun and are better able to be compassionate.

Now onto the fifth and final word of The Five Word Legacy.

Affirmation for Compassion

As I go within myself I know that I am love and joy. I know that happiness is my real nature and is the way I wish to project myself to others. I recognise that I can make the choice to be or not be compassionate towards those I meet. Although deeds and actions that I disagree with occur in the world, I can choose not to judge those around me.

I consider our model of judgement and wonder what value it brings to our world? Judgement does not heal but brings punishment to the world. As I sit in a glow of love and joy, I know I do not want to punish either myself or the world I live in. While not condoning the violent or aggressive actions of others, I wish to show compassion and understanding. I consider these thoughts peacefully and calmly. I prepare myself to live the final word of the legacy in my glory.

7. Word Five - Kindness

"Oh I get by with a little help from my friends."

from: *"I Get By With A Little Help From My Friends"*

Our final gift to the world, the word that makes the other words of the legacy authentic, is kindness. The actions of loving kindness show people that we walk our talk, that we can undertake acts of continual loving kindness in the world. Continual because there is no need to stop being kind, we do not act kindly once or twice, it becomes a way of life that heals the world.

However, kindness is not just about our behaviour or doing kind things. Like the other words of the legacy, kindness comes from the heart and is reflected in our essence of being kind in every feeling, thought and gesture. In the same way as we need to learn to love ourselves, it is just as important to be kind to ourselves.

The word kindness itself is also open to interpretation. We sometimes talk about being kind by undertaking acts of "tough love". Doing things that are "cruel to be kind", believing that doing something perhaps hurtful now may be perceived as an act of kindness in the long run. But will something perceived as cruel now, also be cruel later? For example, a mercy killing. How do the two words sit comfortably in the same sentence – killing is probably perceived as neither kind or merciful?

What can I do to be kind? Ask the question the other way round. What could I do in the situation in which I find myself that is not kind? And why, casting my mind back to the legacy of the other four words, would I choose to undertake an unkind action? This may simply be no action when action is possible. For example, I may hear the screams of the woman (in the previous chapter) being beaten by a stick and not do anything about it. Would that be unkind? All I have to do is call the police and stop a harmful situation, not much to have to do. But I may choose to ignore something I would rather not get involved in.

I could also give money to, or buy a sandwich for, the person begging in the street. I could report a stray dog that is clearly lost and frightened so it is collected and homed. I could smile at the person who has served me at the supermarket checkout, who is probably more tired than I am at the end of a long day. I could choose not to curse the driver who just cut in front of my car on the motorway. I could give time to patiently wait for an elderly person in front of me in the post office queue to be served. I could accept the swearing of young people on the bus without judgement.

The list is endless. Some of these things simply involve my

attitude and do not necessarily involve me in doing anything at all. On other occasions am I being kind in doing nothing? And if I undertake to do something, to what extent is it an act of loving kindness? As I observe situations I must be careful to avoid judgement, especially if it masquerades as compassion. When we talk of a "kind person" we generally mean that he or she is a caring individual. How do we equate kindness with care? Is it the same as being compassionate?

To be kind is a choice. I have a choice to undertake simple kind acts towards other people. Let us look at whether a kind act is also a helpful act. Assisting an elderly person with a shopping bag is helping them in a practical sense. But a smile or a listening ear can brighten someone's day. They are both acts of loving kindness, but to be kind doesn't always involve helping in a material way, we may also be helping in a "feel good" or healing sense. We are "making a difference" and that is never wasted.

Whether people notice my kind gesture or not, being kind will probably make me feel good about me, so reinforce the self-love and joy within me, because I am walking my talk, giving and receiving in a positive way with every action I undertake. As Amelia Earhart says, "A single act of kindness throws out roots in all directions, and the roots spring up and make new trees."

Another type of kindness I may consider is environmental kindness. Not only can I be kind to my fellow human beings, but I can also extend my kindness to all life on our planet by considering my ecological footprint. How much do I waste and how much do I recycle, how many miles do I drive? Walking for example is not only environmentally friendly but enhances our awareness to be in tune with the landscape and connect with the Earth in a simple, sacred and loving way.

We all know there are many actions that help to protect our planet and consume our resources at a slower rate. In making efforts towards this we are caring about our future. This kindness to Mother Earth could be rewarded with less CO_2 emissions, lower planetary temperatures, protection and preservation of wildlife and endangered species, including ourselves.

Indeed, whether we show kindness or undertake a kind action, there is no end to the kindness that we can convey everyday in every way to everyone we encounter. However, we have a choice whether to do this or not.

The Five Word Legacy I have described is entirely based on choice, a personal choice we can all make daily and hourly. It is about choosing to be love and joy and to leave happiness, compassion and kindness wherever we go and in whatever we do.

What legacy would you like the next person you meet to leave you and what will you leave for them?

What might your shopping list of kind choices have on it? There is an abundance of kind choices, no shortage of acts of to be undertaken. A simple choice might be to forgo the purchase of a personal item that you do not really need. Perhaps a personalised number plate for your car and instead make a donation of equal monetary value for a charity that offers clean drinking water to a soul brother or sister we have never met. At our heart level we know we can give from our world of plenty to people in their world of scarce resources knowing that we are all connected by love. To make excuses for why we cannot do this comes from the chattering brain, not the loving heart.

The following chapters will take the five words of the legacy outlined here and apply them to the everyday situations that many of us find ourselves in. We will see how doing this can improve our loving and giving, both for ourselves and for those around us.

Affirmation for Kindness

I breathe in the words of love and joy. As I breathe out happiness and compassion this makes me view the world with eyes full of kindness. There is no shortage to the acts of loving kindness I can perform. I notice the smiles of gratitude that people have for my actions, the way in which they can take such deeds forward to others they meet.

My actions of kindness become the change I want to see for the world I live in. My world needs my help and I offer it willingly knowing that what I give is what I will receive. When I give a smile, I usually receive a smile in return. When I help another person, animal or plant a feeling of selflessness rewards me. To be kind is not a chore; it is a gift. I am thankful for the gifts I give myself.

As my kind deeds are undertaken, I notice the generosity of others who want to do the same for me. As I give and I receive, healing the world can happen. The choice to partake in this healing becomes mine.

8. Legacy In Family

"She breaks down and cries to her husband, 'daddy our baby's gone'."

from: *"She's Leaving Home"*

Most of us are born into a family and many of us go on to raise a family of our own. For many people the desire to create a family, with a partner and children, is a driving force in their lives. To have a home, job, income, education for the children, money to buy toys for adults and children, and have as much worldly pleasure as can be achieved in the material world is what is aspired to.

However, it is apparent that many families do not derive pleasure or satisfaction from all that they accumulate in a material sense. There may be arguments and rows and painful upsets that divide families. This may leave some members deeply hurt or isolated and wishing they did not belong in that family;

that if only they lived somewhere else everything would be all right. Does this sound familiar?

Whether it is a parent, child, grandparent, aunt, uncle, niece, nephew, step-child, step-parent or any other combination that may make up a family, they may live together harmoniously or may be fragmented, fractured or just plain broken. With high divorce rates and the amalgamation of families from previous relationships, we see a melting pot of inter-relational arrangements where children may live under more than one roof, perhaps with dad at one home and mum and her new partner at another. There may be children of more than one parental relationship living in the same house, all trying to get on with one another (or perhaps not) and attempting to live a "normal" life.

Being a family member involves consideration of others; life is not just about us. This can be stressful; many things may happen in a day, week, month or year that means the family unit is challenged. Perhaps the greatest challenge is how the family behaves and reacts when something goes "wrong". Is there high drama with loud words and great upset, is blame attached, is someone made to feel guilty, is there a price to be paid by the family whenever things are not "right"? As you read this you may recall similar situations in your own family, either as a child, or in the family situation you are currently in.

Similarly, when things simmer down, does the family group take a similar view of the situation or are individuals made to feel isolated as a result? Is the general attitude one of judgement or does the bigger picture prevail; was it a rather petty incident in the scheme of things, perhaps something happening for a reason? Few of us like change, anything that "rocks our boat", yet to become complacent within a family lifestyle in which negative patterns prevail – our own or those of others, some of whom we may not have chosen to have to "get on" with – is both unhealthy and can give rise to dis-ease.

The debate about what is normal family life could last a long time. However, it would be good to ask, "Are we a happy family?" How can we create healthy and happy families?

Now that you have read this far, you know what it takes to be happy and to have the internal love and joy that was described earlier. If you have that happiness can you recognise the same "inner glow" in others within your family? It may be that some of your family members have it and some do not. It might be good if more than just yourself has the same understanding and expression of happiness within the family, because you can then link and harness together this same positive energy. It may be at this time that only you are able to convey happy energy fuelled by love and joy. If that is the case, remember you will need courage to behave with loving kindness.

Either way, this may be the time to consider adopting The Five Word Legacy in your family. You may feel that to have these five words as the values you will all live by is what you wish to do, but the question may then be "How?" Can we all live by the same values, what if someone says this is not for them?

It may be that to begin with you are a lone voice and others within your family are not prepared to adopt a new way of looking at the world that you feel will lead to family harmony – or at least improve your situation from how it is at present. They may not wish to undertake the journey you have taken towards internal love and joy. These are the two steps that will allow each family member to join you in that "Ready Brek" state towards bliss. However, trying to force people to agree with you and undertake something before they are ready will probably not work. So what can you do instead?

Firstly, you can continue your own life journey using The Five Word Legacy. Do not be put off or distracted by the influences of others. Use courage to remain centred and true to the belief that you are a shining and wonderful person, entitled and privileged to live by such high values. Be a beacon or lighthouse, that is to say be a shining example of who you are and what your values represent, show happiness at every opportunity to everyone in your family. You do not have to condone behaviour that is disruptive to a healthy family dynamic, but do not allow it to consume you or "rock your boat". Remain sufficiently detached so that you can be calm and happy. Use honest words to describe your feelings, but deliver them with compassion. If you wound another with your words, you wound yourself and you will realise an opportunity to be kind has been missed.

What will being a lone beacon in the dark achieve? It may mean that others in the family view you with suspicion, test you and set you up in an attempt to make you fail. Living a new lifestyle in your new legacy, your family will not be able to help notice this change in you, especially if you had less positive behaviour patterns in the past. They may have the feeling that your new-found way of living is too good to be true and try to get you to revert back to old habits.

There is a great human value you can use everyday to help you achieve your goal of adopting your own legacy, and also to help others to achieve theirs. This value is courage. It is important to remember that you will need this. A word we all know, but what does it mean? Courage is often seen at its best in the face of fear.

When we are afraid because the challenge ahead seems too great or the price too high we may be tempted to forget who we are in relation to others, our compassion and kindness may elude us. We may worry that we may experience pain, lose respect or feel humiliated for living our legacy and not conforming to the expectations of others.

At this point of reading you may have realised that having found the love and joy of the legacy you do not want to give it up. So a choice presents itself, live steadfast in your newfound truth, or return to being influenced by the emotions of others who seemingly dictate how you should feel and act. This is a simple choice, but perhaps not an easy one. It could be one of the hardest decisions you make. However, the beauty of having the choice is that you can make the choice to live the legacy at any time.

If at this moment in time you feel that the legacy and its rewards are not possible for you, then in one second's time – the Holy Instant, the "get over it right now" moment – you can choose again, or even sooner. Try it, right now!

Any relationship that you have, whether it is with yourself, your family, or your community – indeed with anyone or anything – is worth taking a second to change your mind, to change your life and the lives of others. If you have just done this, well done, what a courageous commitment you have just made. If you have not, yet, note the "not yet", what will you do in the next second and the second after that? Lots of second chances (get it?), the sooner you get it the sooner you can live it.

Affirmation for Family

With my breathing calm and relaxed, I consider my own feelings towards my family, how I felt about family members when I was a child and how they affected me as I grew up. Did my family live any of the words of The Five Word Legacy? Do I recall happiness being shown to me, was compassion and kindness present in the home where I grew up? How do I feel about my family now in this very moment?

I may not have chosen my immediate family: my parents, brothers, sisters and other relatives. I may not have always shared their beliefs and values, but they are my family. I can choose how I respond to my family; I can share with them all the words of The Five Word Legacy and courageously "be" the essence of loving kindness towards them.

If there are feelings of resentment, guilt, anger or pain towards any member of my family, I acknowledge them now. I don't try to hide them, but realise that these feelings were my previous truth and now I can exchange those feelings for compassion and kindness. I breathe deeply and slowly, relaxing more and more with each breath as I recall each member of my family with love. Even if I have been hurt or abused by someone in my family, I remember that I am loving joy. I know that if I do not forgive any family member for whom I harbour resentment or for whom I hold the memory of pain, then I place a barrier to my ability "to be" loving joy. I am my own lock and my own key to joy.

I take a moment, just a second to be the change I wish to be in my family. Knowing that I can love my family and myself in equal measure.

9. Legacy At Work

"It's been a hard day's night and I've been working like a dog."

from: *"Hard Day's Night"*

What does the workplace mean to you? Is it where you go to earn a living, the main focus being your wages, career progression, or being with colleagues? Perhaps work is a means to an end for you or perhaps it is all that you live for and gives your life meaning. Some people may be very excited at the prospect of going to work each day, some may dread it, or for others there may be a stressful feeling of being burnt out and having had enough, unable to wait to leave a particular environment, occupation or to retire.

What relevance can The Five Word Legacy have in the workplace? Unless we work from home, the place where we earn our living can often be a strange or unfamiliar environment. Many people "go out" to work. For some this may bring relief if home is not a happy place. Others may desire to return home in every moment they are at work. Whichever view we have, as adults we will usually spend many years needing to work. While the traditional eight hours a day, five days a week, now offers greater flexibility, our work will generally involve responsibilities, tasks and duties in the employ of someone else to earn our wages to support our families and ourselves.

Within an environment that may be your version of heaven or hell, how do you behave on a daily basis? Do you skip happily to work only to stop when you arrive because you feel you must behave in a different way, be a different person? Perhaps you feel you cannot be the true you at work; that you need to wear armour or present yourself differently because you must conform or play a certain role. It may be that in your workplace a demanding boss or colleague makes you feel inadequate or less confident than you want to feel. Again, we are in the territory of being influenced more by others than by our own inner sense of well-being.

In case there is any doubt, The Five Word Legacy is not confined to where and when we can use it. You will recall from earlier that it is for always and in all ways. Also remember that you may need courage in old and familiar places, including your workplace, to be your new found self and to be able to express yourself happily, compassionately and kindly at work.

There are so many ways you can be kind at work. If a colleague is crying or having a bad day, you may provide a tissue, a cup of tea, a hug, or the time to listen. You do not even have to like that person. The legacy teaches you to love yourself enough in order to be giving to this colleague so that you naturally and unconditionally love everyone you encounter. Whether in need or not, someone will receive your kindness because you are happy to be compassionate towards him or her. Even if you work in an environment where displays of personal feeling are not encouraged and hugs and tissues are not on the agenda, a smile in your voice as you say "good morning" in person or on the telephone can make all the difference. Try it, please, just break old habits and give all the loving kindness that you can.

If you are a manager or hold a senior position in your workplace are there ways to make large-scale differences to your workforce, your customers, the community and the environment? For anyone in a position with any form of corporate influence, then the answer cannot be "no". Any attempt to improve relationships and your business does not suggest that you are ineffectual in your job role. However, in any interaction with others and when any decision needs to be made, can your business brain relate to the person or situation with a compassionate heart? All communication and decisions can be blended and shaped to be as kind as possible. Again, try it, please, the next chance you get, which may be quite soon.

What if you cannot see any reason or have any wish to do things differently? You need another "second chance". The things that may hold us back are going to be varied. You may wonder, "How can I show I am happy in a job that I do not like, or even loathe?" Such resistance to demonstrating happiness is not unusual, but is a waste of a precious opportunity. Remember the sequence of the words of the legacy. Before compassion and kindness comes the genuine demonstration to others that you are happy. If you cannot do that in the workplace then it is time to be still, and to know that you are the inner love and joy for yourself; that is your protection from the pain that you may have experienced in the world of work, or sadness in your life that may be reflected in your personality and behaviour in the workplace.

There may also be other obstacles that hold us back such as ego, arrogance, pride, or previous hurts and insults that we cannot forgive or forget. All of these are barriers that prevent the legacy becoming true for oneself, and also for others – those we are here to serve. Because once the legacy is within you, all you will want to do is share it with others.

Previous roles and responsibilities, previous hurts and insults from work colleagues, managers, customers or anyone else that you felt "owned" you at work will in some way, large or small, be influenced by you and your legacy. Remember that it will take time and courage for The Five Word Legacy to become second nature to you, an integral part of your being. Sometimes one or more of the words may not come easily at first; how we feel about ourselves will reflect the legacy we choose to share.

Here is an example. If you change The Five Word Legacy from "Love, Joy, Happiness, Compassion, Kindness" to the following five words: "Hate, Fear, Misery, Unfeeling, Uncaring", what happens? Everything changes. Love and joy cannot be within you and therefore cannot be with others, no matter who they are. How we think and feel about ourselves will determine our actions and behaviour towards others. We are just as worthy of loving ourselves as the next person. And the more positive we can feel about ourselves the better empowered we will be to share our loving kindness in unconditional ways with others. The legacy is about encouraging all of us to dispense with negative words and feelings and adopt positive expressions, to "be the change" from within.

The loving kindness you give through your legacy cannot be

shown to some and not to others, it is for all. We do not ration the air that we breathe, so why ration or select who deserves the beauty of your legacy? Give it openly and freely in every work situation. Take heart and take courage, you will live a richer life for it … and eventually so will everyone you meet.

This will mean that the place in which you work will have at least one beacon in it – that is you – the most important person to you. Plus once you start to shine you will see other shining lights in your colleagues and wonder why you never saw them before. The sky overhead in your workplace may be grey, but the colour of your own sky is a choice you can make.

Affirmation for my Workplace

In a state of relaxed calm I consider my workplace. How do I feel about where I work and the people I work with? What reaction does my body and mind have to my work? Are there good feelings about what I do, and about my colleagues? What if there are not good feelings?

I take time to consider these feelings and accept them. I consider what I can do to bring meaningful change to any negative feelings I have about work. Is there a change that I can choose?

Do I want to approach my work and my colleagues with greater kindness? Do I wish to find a way to feel more satisfied with the actual tasks I undertake? Or is it time to bring a change to where I work and what I do? Is my highest self given the chance to grow and expand at work, not just in the tasks that I perform, but also in my interactions with others?

I affirm to myself that even when work is boring, tedious or stressful I can use The Five Word Legacy for myself and others. I will share my loving joy with a smile, a kind word or a small gesture that will bring happiness to others. The very next time I am at work, I will not delay.

10. Legacy At School

"Monday's child has learned to tie his shoe lace."

from: *"Lady Madonna"*

It has been a long time since I was at school. However, my memories of the all boy secondary modern school I went to have stayed with me as an unpleasant experience. The legacy of Love, Joy, Happiness, Compassion and Kindness had little to do with the constant bullying I witnessed and at times received from others.

Today, in more enlightened times, our schools are nurturing places for children to flourish and express themselves freely and openly without peer pressure or bullying; aren't they? The answer for many is sadly "no", so what place does The Five Word Legacy have within our educational system?

At what age do we feel a child is young enough to receive our spiritual wisdom? When do we consider sharing our guidance with our children? Could it be from conception when that tiny spark of life is receiving stimuli in the womb of its mother? Learning never starts and stops, it continues every day of our lives and is a constant in our lives. Even when consciously "not" learning we are learning something about the world we live in and the way we react to it.

What role does school play for children, whether it is nursery or sixth form? Perhaps the best people to ask are those for whom school is for, our children, whether they are primary, high school or college pupils and students. But do we? Do we design an educational system with the spiritual growth of young people at the forefront of our minds? Do we consult children about their needs and encourage them to be loving and kind pupils within our world? I suspect not.

In the United Kingdom and many other countries, the focus of education appears to be purely towards the attainment of qualifications for the purposes of employment as an adult. We do not appear to guide our children's growth and development upon a legacy. There are however some exceptional schools, teachers and parents who encourage each child as an individual to reach his or her potential and focus on awareness of human values. Student teachers *are* taught about the five important areas of child development: physical, intellectual, emotional, moral and social. However, with today's schools concentrating on meeting academic targets, important areas of development are frequently overlooked in the demands of "the system".

Increasingly high rates of childhood obesity, smoking,

alcohol consumption and pregnancy suggest that children want to experiment with a number of the vices that life has to offer. Or do they? Are these outcomes simply the result of boredom, lack of healthier stimulating alternatives in a more creative environment or of ignorance?

Children and teenagers naturally seek experiences that involve taking risks, because with risk taking comes new sensations (some pleasurable and some not). Some of these behaviours can be potentially addictive; we take the risks to have the sensations and repeat the behaviours to continue having the sensations. Such entrenched habits may be carried into adult life, a short-term "buzz" that steers us away from the delights that are offered by The Five Word Legacy.

What can our education system do to prevent destructive behaviours that can lead to addiction? Perhaps, just perhaps, the key lies with our schools and with their teachers. Could The Five Word Legacy become part of our curriculum? Especially important are our nursery and primary schools when we remember the wisdom of the Jesuits who asserted, "Give me a child until he is seven, and I will show you the man." Could teachers be so full of love and joy at being teachers in such an esteemed and privileged position, that our positive legacy spills into happiness in the teachers' workplace *and* our children's place of learning.

What a win-win for our society that could be. What if any behaviour of our children in the classroom was met with a response of "what would love do next?" We recognise that some behaviour of children is difficult and at times dangerous, and that teaching can be stressful and burn out can be high. However, if we can protect our teachers, reward them for their efforts and not criticise when not all standards of school performance are met. If we can place the same value on developing emotional, moral, social and spiritual awareness as we do to achievement in terms of grades. If we can respect our children as equals, not inferior or subservient because of age, race, faith or any other stigma, while also appreciating that they need the wisdom of our support and guidance. A lot of "ifs" … but if these can be met then we can begin to offer a truly educational experience that will reward our children, the world we all inhabit, and ourselves.

As I write this, fully aware of the limitations of referring to the complex subject of education in a few short paragraphs, I am reminded of the work of musician James Twyman. In 1994 he began taking prayers from all the main religions of the world to war-torn countries, the goal of his concerts was "to demonstrate that all spiritual paths point to a single expression" – that of Love. During his "Peace Troubadour" ministry, he met some extraordinary children who taught him that we all have a gift within us; it just needs to be awakened. They asked the following question:

> *"What would the world be like if we all realized that we are Emissaries of Love right now?*

What would a child or an adolescent "emissary of light" be like, and what would their aspirations be? In our Westernised society many young people succumb to powerful media advertising and stereotyping, behaving in ways that may have little to do with light and inner wisdom. The words of The Five Word Legacy may not have meaning during these formative years.

To create a society that honours the young we must show them respect from birth as souls with an equal right to express views and opinions; and engage them in activities and discussion between extended families, teachers and others. This integrated approach can help us to share loving kindness. There is then no place for bullying or discrimination because someone is "different". Through example, we can encourage our children to embrace all life and to create a world that is safe and secure for all.

It is failing in our responsibility to consider that our children are our future if we do not equip them with the values and the tools that allow them to build a future based on love, courage, trust and respect. Do we believe that if as adults we do not demonstrate such values now in this present moment that millions of young people will inherit a legacy of loving kindness to use in the future? To give of our time and to listen is crucial if we are to nurture those on whom the future of our society and the Earth depends. Our planet and its inhabitants will reap the future fruit of the seeds that we sow now.

The following affirmation is to help us guide and support our young people.

Affirmation for Schools

In a state of relaxation and contemplation, I ponder my own school experiences. What were they like, how did they make me feel, what did I gain from my schooling? Do the positive experiences still serve me today, or did school create obstacles that prevent me from achieving my full abilities?

I know that most children I encounter will attend schools. I consider how I can encourage and support (without interfering) the development of children that I know in their formative years. Can I be an inspiration for children who may be struggling at school because they find study hard, are being bullied, or find school difficult for another reason? Are they open to receive the wisdom I have to offer?

Through my use of The Five Word Legacy, which words will I focus on to devote my energy to the development of a particular child or adolescent? What legacy can I leave for them? Can we focus on encouraging our children to open their hearts and believe that they too are "Emissaries of Love"?

11. Legacy In Relationships

*"And in the end, the love you take
is equal to the love you make."*

from: *"Golden Slumbers/The End"*

We have many types of relationships in our lives. Some have already been touched upon on this legacy journey. However, those now referred to are the people in our relationships who are, or have been, closest to us in an emotional way, a way that touches our hearts and brings us pleasure and perhaps also pain.

Those who influence us most are often a parent, spouse, partner, boyfriend, girlfriend, lover, best friend, soul mate or any other term you may wish to use. The use of The Five Word Legacy is easy when a relationship functions well and two people join their five words together and make ten words acting in harmony on a daily basis. Therefore we will not dwell on harmonious relationships, because words are not required when all is well. However, when relationships lose their harmony, what can we do?

For many of us, when we believe we have "fallen in love" then the relationship can become all-consuming. All rule books can go out of the window. In any relationship, while it is fun, caring and supportive, all is well. But what happens when the boat is rocked? Perhaps by a row or an argument, or a shift in feelings for one person and not the other? Someone or something better comes along, all manner of reasons why the relationship shifts. This may involve our own perception of that person, or some kind of change within our self. Without a solid internal foundation our emotions are no longer at our control, but are under the influence of someone or something else.

You are back in the storm in a tea cup situation, unable to think or feel in your best way, you are trying to hang on to the sides of the cup, trying to manage fear, pain, doubt and uncertainty. You may believe that the other person in the relationship is the person who decides what happens and when, that you are disempowered until they make a decision for you.

This may sound extreme, but if you have ever felt pain because of a relationship, what was the cause? Were you able to control the reason and thus prevent the pain, or did you have a time of such suffering that you felt it may never end? Some people may say, "no, I have never felt such pain and never will." Are you the person who can skip to the next chapter or is there some internal work to do within your relationships?

If you decided to stick with this chapter then let us go a little deeper, because the feelings from relationship can be the most wonderful feelings we can experience in our lives. Let us explore ways that allow that to be so.

With family members, such as a parent or sibling, we may have a blood tie. With others, such as meeting a stranger who comes into our lives, what creates the bond of friendship or potential to become a lover? Why are we attracted to another person? Every person we meet creates possibilities for us; reactions at both ends of the spectrum such as like/dislike, love/hate or obsession/disinterest. What we may experience can depend on a number of factors.

Assuming we are looking for a relationship and want to accept a friend or lover into our lives there may be two main reasons. One may be that we seek to have a need met by another, perhaps because of a fear or insecurity that we want sated, healed or nursed by someone other than ourselves. This can be like a toxic residue that we carry around in the hope that another person can wash it off for us. We are externally needy and want another to heal or rescue us.

The other more beneficial reason may be that having adopted The Five Word Legacy, we have developed the internal tools to be love and to be joy for ourselves. While we are self-sufficient and responsible, we also recognise the areas of our life that are unhealed, which we are still working on or struggling with.

Throughout our lives we are given more and more opportunities for personal growth. Sometimes similar situations will come around again and again, recurring patterns that we may recognise but not necessarily know what to do about them. Childhood memories of rejection, sibling rivalry, early relationships that ended badly, are all experiences that may have resulted in resentment or a lack of trust. Sometimes we may be set in our ways, conditioned to respond in a certain way because of our upbringing. This is different from, for example, reacting to a tragic event in a way dictated to us by cinema and television. For many of us, repeat scenarios may play out in our most intimate personal relationships; we may feel they will never end, but then they do. We have been allowed to try again, to heal that which remains unresolved inside us.

When a relationship has broken up, we may feel that the loss we have had is too great to recover from, that we will fall apart and never be healed. Our loss may be great, the person we have lost may well be equally hurt and lost, not sure of what to do next. So what can we do?

Let us apply the legacy. Can we love ourselves enough and retain a sense of self-worth? Something important has been lost, but not everything – we are still blessed in many ways. We have air in our lungs, some degree of health, and may have friends willing to support us and provide healing. It is essential that we retain the love of ourselves. When we can respect ourselves with love, we can also love the one we have lost. This will be a very hard challenge especially if the other person ended the relationship and you did not want to break-up. But if you cannot love that person then other feelings that are not love, such as anger, shame and resentment will prevail and become consuming.

Let us use another word of the legacy, compassion. Can you be compassionate towards the other person as well as yourself? Are you the victim of the lost relationship? Do you see the other as the perpetrator of your pain? Remember to show compassion to victim and perpetrator in equal measure? Again not easy as this may be a new way of feeling, thinking and acting after such an event.

In the past, did you cry, feel terrible sadness and apportion blame to the other? Or did you have these same feelings projected towards you? How did those judgemental feelings serve you, did they aid your recovery or hinder and slow it down? When you are in a state of distress it may be that others around you also show empathy for your situation by agreeing with your anguish or resentment. This can have the opposite effect to that intended and reinforce your sadness. Others may be like an angel by your side and help to guide you out of the mire. You can be like the lotus flower that floats on top of muddy water rather than wallowing in it.

There is a time to grieve and a time to rise above feelings that cannot aid your recovery. Once compassion has become a part of you, the road to kindness is not far away. Kindness to yourself, a time to be gentle and accepting of your loss, knowing that it is acceptable to have feelings that are sad. It is also important to recall times of happiness and acknowledge what the relationship gave you and what you gave to the relationship. No time or effort was wasted because you gave what you felt was the best you could give at that time, as did your partner(s) in the relationship.

So you can step away from judgement, use compassion to remind yourself of your happiness and again undertake acts of kindness towards your partner, even if all you can manage is the ability to say to yourself, "I forgive what happened and love myself." You can then move forward on life's journey, content that you can love, be joyful and happy while viewing the world with compassion and kindness.

Affirmation for Relationships

Once more as I deepen my breath and consider myself with love, my joy is awakened within me and I am calm.

I turn my attention to my relationships, perhaps towards someone with whom I share myself, or with another from the past. Which words of The Five Word Legacy do I use to affirm myself to the person I am relating to?

What form does my love take? I affirm to make my love truthful, open and unconditional to myself and in my relationship. I am filled with joy when I am with my other. I demonstrate joy to myself and allow it to spill into my relationship in the form of happiness. My partner senses my happiness and is able to respond by being uplifted.

When things go wrong, I do not judge the behaviour of myself or of my partner. Instead, I set aside the time to go within and find my compassion. This allows me to forgive the event that has caused me hurt. As my focus is not on forgiving my partner, the relationship carries on without the burden of judgement.

I am kind towards my partner at every opportunity. This is reciprocated with the same level of kindness. We share mutual respect and honour each other as beautiful, caring individuals who have chosen to be a part of each other's lives.

12. In Your Own Words

"I've got a feeling, deep inside, oh yeah."

from: *"I've Got A Feeling"*

I have described my Five Word Legacy, what it means to me and how that may be shared with others. However, you may feel very differently about the same five words, indeed you may have other words that have a particular significance or feeling for you.

You may wish to consider which words resonate *within you* such as "Love" and "Joy", and which words you *express to others* in the same way as "Happiness", "Compassion" and "Kindness". The reason for the sequence of these words is firstly, for our inner being to know it is alive, and secondly, for the outer delivery of our being to others.

61

As a reminder, here are simple definitions of the five words:

Love	To hold dear
Joy	A source of delight
Happiness	To bring pleasure
Compassion	To consciously care and alleviate distress
Kindness	The state of being kind

My website www.thefivewordlegacy.co.uk has a page where people have left many different suggestions of words that they use and choose to live by.

These words capture an essence to serve the highest ways of being: Loving Kindness. They carry an energy that uplifts our spirits. Not all of the following are five words, but the intention is there:

Acceptance - intention - creation - evolution - transformation

Truth * Conscious * Creative * Being * Freedom

Peace...Love...Light...Spirit...Hope

Love trust respect faith belief

Sparkling Conscious Wonderment Loving Kindness

one is definitely DIGNITY and another would be GRACE

Laughter, Believe, Family, Peace and Hope

Love, hope, acceptance, kindness and happiness

Love, hope, compassion, empathy and patience

Hang on to your hat!

There must be thousands more, why not add your own comments?

Of greater importance, search within yourself and find five words that you believe are imperative to define who you are and what you believe. This inner truth is the foundation of who you are today and will help to live a life of loving kindness with no effort at all.

Perhaps your words will change over the days and weeks, months and years ahead. That is fine. The one constant we are likely to experience in life is change. Will your five words make change a pleasure for you, or reflect a storm in your tea cup?

I truly hope that your own five words will become part of your own personal legacy, and that The Five Word Legacy I have been inspired to share with you will enrich your lives for the better and help spread happiness and healing to all around you.

Finally ... we are told that we are sent no one or no thing but angels, that everyone and everything is a gift. We can only act "now" in the present – that is why it is called a gift. Therefore, whomever we meet and whatever we experience has the potential to move us on our spiritual journey ... unless we feel it does not and we decide to choose again.

That is the beauty of life, free will and the ability to change at any moment we choose, unless we choose not to. Then, when we do, the dance of life moves on.

Namaste

"The spirit in me recognises the spirit in you and we are one."

Acknowledgements

The following authors and their books/quotations have been used with my thanks to help me in this illustration of The Five Word Legacy:

Saint Francis of Assisi. Prayer: *"Lord, make me an instrument of your peace."*
The Holy Bible (King James' vers.), *The Old Testament, Psalm 46. Mark, chapter 12: verse 31.*
The Buddha. *The Dhammapada, the path of perfection.* Translated by Juan Mascaro, Penguin Classics,1973.
Lewis Carroll. *Alice In Wonderland,* Penguin Classics, 1865.
A Course in Miracles, The Foundation for Inner Peace, 1975.
Amelia Earhart. Quote: *"A single act of kindness."*
Dr Masaru Emoto. *The Hidden Messages in Water,* Beyond Words Publishing Company, 2004.
Mohandas Gandhi. Quote: *"Happiness is when what you think."*
Oriah Mountain Dreamer. *The Call,* Element Books, 2004.
Rumi. c1300 Quote: *"O Love, O pure deep Love, be here, be now."*
James F Twyman. *Emissary of Light,* Warner Books, 1998.

Useful Resources

Our world is full of resources to help us to build a legacy for ourselves and for others in our spiritual journey. Libraries, bookshops, music, and most of all the internet, are full of material that can enrich lives and assist people to move along their spiritual pathway.

Here are a number of suggestions that may help you in your quest:

Authors:

The Buddha
Roger Cole
The Dalai Lama
Dr Marc Gafni
Dadi Janki
Sister Jayanti
C S Lewis
Rudolf Steiner
Neale Donald Walsch
Paul M Young

Organisations:

Bramha Kumaris World Spiritual University, www.bkwsu.org
Center for World Spirituality, www.ievolve.org
The Conversations with God Foundation, www.cwg.org
A Course in Miracles, http://acim.org/index.html
The Five Word Legacy, www.thefivewordlegacy.co.uk
Humanities Team, http://www.humanitysteam.org
Interfaith Foundation, www.interfaithfoundation.org

Singers and Musicians:

The Beatles
Bliss
Crowded House
Lucinda Drayton
Bob Marley
Margaret Owens
Roma Waterman

The author Noel Lockyer-Stevens is an Interfaith Minister who lives a vow "to love myself and others, while on life's journey".

He explains how we can all live positive and fulfilling lives without effort and share the wonder of each moment with others – a simple and vital mission for humanity.

Noel lives in Dorset, UK and is available for consultations, spiritual support, ceremonies and talks.

www.thefivewordlegacy.co.uk

66

www.ingramcontent.com/pod-product-compliance
Lightning Source LLC
LaVergne TN
LVHW021544080426
835509LV00019B/2834

9 7 8 0 9 5 6 1 8 8 6 8 7